AF423224

Arming the Union

Gunmakers in Windsor, Vermont

Brady.
Life in Camp Cameron Washington
May 1861

Arming the Union

Gunmakers in Windsor, Vermont

Carrie Brown, Ph.D.

American Precision Museum
Windsor, Vermont
2012

This essay first appeared in the journal *Vermont History*, in the Summer/Fall 2011 issue. It appears here with permission of the Vermont Historical Society. APM gratefully acknowledges the support of both the journal and the Historical Society.

William Hale Foster letters are quoted courtesy of the descendants of William and Maria Foster.

Frontispiece: Life in Camp Cameron, Matthew Brady, 1861, courtesy of the Library of Congress.

This version published by
American Precision Museum
Windsor, Vermont
2012

Foreword

Carrie Brown's article casts fresh light not only on Vermont's industrial contribution to the Union's victory during the Civil War, but also the town of Windsor as an exemplar of "best practice" in the new field of precision manufacturing. Firms like Robbins & Lawrence and its successor, Lamson, Goodnow & Yale, stood at the forefront of the emerging machine tool industry in the Connecticut Valley. From them came Jones & Lamson and other industry leaders in the late nineteenth and twentieth centuries. Windsor's story thus nicely encapsulates how the United States emerged as the world's greatest industrial nation during this period. One leaves the article with an enhanced appreciation of Windsor as a seedbed of the "American system of manufactures" and why the area around it became well known as "the Precision Valley." In short, an excellent contribution well worth reading, indeed close study.

Merritt Roe Smith
Leverett and William Cutten Professor of the History of Technology
Massachusetts Institute of Technology
Cambridge, Massachusetts

Civil War-era machinist at the Colt armory,
courtesy of the Connecticut State Library.

Arming the Union

Gunmakers in Windsor, Vermont

Henry David Stone had, metaphorically, beaten the swords into plowshares only a few years earlier. In the three-story brick factory building on Main Street in Windsor, a gun-making firm known as Robbins & Lawrence had designed and built state-of-the-art machines to make guns for the U.S. war with Mexico in the 1840s and for Britain's conflict in the Crimea in the early 1850s. When those wars ended, the machines—and some of the men who operated them—were set to work making parts for sewing machines and other peacetime products. Stone had helped design a double-thread sewing machine known as Clark's Revolving Looper, and he was supervising the work of producing it in 1859 and '60. Then, the secession of seven southern states during the winter of 1860-61, followed by the attack on Fort Sumter in April, brought a new war. Stone now needed to convert the entire operation in Windsor back to guns, gun parts, and gun-making machinery.

Sales records for the Windsor armory—recently uncovered at the American Precision Museum—make it possible to assess what effect this one firm, in a small town in Vermont, had on the war at large. The impact would be enormous.

The Civil War brought unprecedented—almost unimaginable—bloodshed to America. In one day, at the Battle of Antietam, 23,000 Americans were killed, wounded, or missing, and about 4,000 died immediately—more than on any other single day in our history.[1] At Gettysburg, over the course of only three days, there were 50,000 casualties. As Drew Gilpin Faust has pointed out, the number of soldiers who died in the Civil War—about 620,000, north and south—totaled about two per cent of the American population at the time, the equivalent of six million today.[2] True, historians estimate that about two-thirds of them died of disease, but that means that more than 200,000 died of battle wounds.[3]

Many scholars have noted that the high casualties can be blamed partly on new weapons, more deadly than those that had been common in previous wars.[4] One of the most important advances was the rifled gun barrel, which first became practical during the mid 1800s. Rifling—the cutting of spiral grooves inside the barrel—causes the bullet to spin,

"The Army of the Potomac—A Sharpshooter on Picket Duty," Winslow Homer, courtesy of the Smithsonian American Art Museum.

4

greatly increasing its stability and, therefore, the gun's accuracy. The Minié ball, developed in France in 1847, loaded more quickly than older rifle ammunition and was specifically designed to "catch" in those spiral grooves. While smoothbore muskets used by infantrymen in the Napoleonic Wars had an effective range of only about 100 yards, the rifled muskets of the Civil War were effective at 500 yards.[5] Some recent scholarship suggests that this increased range was more theoretical than real, and that Civil War battles took place at approximately the same range as battles in the Napoleonic Wars.[6] But even these scholars would acknowledge that at least the snipers and sharpshooters had a lethal benefit with the new rifles.

The Civil War also saw development of breech-loading weapons, which could be re-loaded and fired more rapidly than the standard muzzle-loader. By the end of the war, repeating weapons had appeared. The new weapons eventually inspired new tactics: fewer cavalry charges, artillery stationed at a greater distance from the enemy to avoid artillerymen picked off by sharpshooters, less movement of masses of men across a battlefield, the development of trench warfare. But the tactics did not evolve quickly enough to avoid terrible carnage.[7]

Clearly, new weapons did change warfare. But another factor also drove the casualty numbers up: the sheer number of men *armed.* More than two million northerners and more than 800,000 southerners served.[8] At the beginning of the war, most men on both sides carried old smoothbore weapons; but by mid-1863, they were armed with new, rifled muskets and carbines.[9] By Flayderman's count, more than a million and a half .58 caliber rifled muskets were made in the North during the war.[10] Richard Colton of the Springfield Armory estimates that the Confederacy manufactured 107,000 shoulder arms and imported more than 340,000.[11] Tens of thousands of pistols were also produced. How was it possible, in the course of two or three years in the early 1860s, to put that many weapons into the field?[12]

The answer lies in a network of machines and machinists that stretched across the northeastern states, with branches extending into the south and across the Atlantic, and with a strong, flourishing branch in Windsor, Vermont. As one of the teams that perfected the methods of "armory

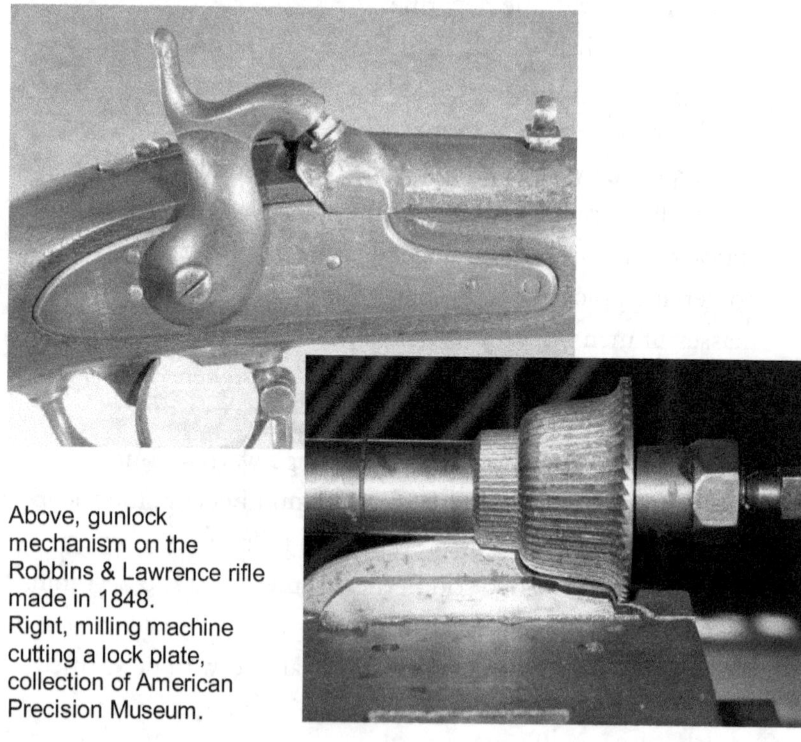

Above, gunlock mechanism on the Robbins & Lawrence rifle made in 1848.
Right, milling machine cutting a lock plate, collection of American Precision Museum.

6

practice," Robbins & Lawrence had designed and built extremely accurate machine tools—milling machines, lathes, drill presses—that could produce gun parts, one after another, all alike and interchangeable.

Robbins & Lawrence did not independently "invent" the new machinery. Gunmakers, especially those in the federal armories at Harper's Ferry, Virginia, and Springfield, Massachusetts, had been working toward interchangeability since the late eighteenth century. Open-door policies in the government armories and among government contractors helped spread the improvements in machinery and systems. Machinists moved from one shop to another, developing friendships, mentoring the young, and steadily improving the tools. With the Ordnance Department insisting upon precision metal cutting and efficient systems of production— and bankrolling the developing technology—new methods and machines evolved rapidly in the early nineteenth century. By midcentury, it would be possible for a single factory to produce as many as a thousand guns a month.[13]

In Windsor, Robbins, Kendall, & Lawrence (later simply Robbins & Lawrence) won a contract in 1846 for 10,000 rifles for the United States government. After finishing that order early, the firm received a second contract, for another 15,000 guns. Improving upon existing tools, adding their own innovations, and perfecting the methods of precision manufacturing, Robbins & Lawrence became a model for the new system. Contracts with the British for Enfield rifles and for machines to outfit Britain's Enfield Armory followed in the 1850s. American gun makers were also purchasing Robbins & Lawrence machines. Letters from the mid-1850s detail sales of a universal milling machine to the Springfield Armory; a drill press to Remington & Sons in Illion, New York; gun sights to Eli Whitney, Jr.; and rifling machines to a firm in Chicopee, Massachusetts.[14] Mid-nineteenth-century photographs from Samuel Colt's factory in Hartford show what are almost certainly a Robbins & Lawrence milling machine and drill press. As the company developed more products, the size of the operation grew, and more buildings went up on both sides of Mill Brook in Windsor.

Universal milling machine designed in 1858 at Robbins & Lawrence in Windsor, Vermont, collection of American Precision Museum.

8

Robbins & Lawrence universal
milling machine at the Colt
factory in Hartford, Connecticut,
around 1860, from a glass plate
photograph, courtesy of the
Connecticut State Library.

In the annals of the machine tool industry, Windsor innovators Richard Lawrence and Frederick W. Howe are better remembered than Henry Stone, and Howe was certainly the most brilliant machine designer of the group. Nonetheless, Stone's contributions were significant. In 1854, he developed a new rifling machine for making what he called "the English gun"—the Enfield rifle.[15] This machine could cut the long, precise spiral grooves all day long without tiring and without erring. And so Henry Stone helped proliferate those new rifled muskets that would prove so deadly in the 1860s.

Stone had also worked with Howe on lathes to turn bayonets, and on a profile milling machine that could cut complex shapes such as gun triggers and lock plates. These profile milling, or "edging," machines were supplied to the Enfield Armory, and similar machines were made at the Springfield Armory, from Robbins & Lawrence drawings.[16] Most of the extant shop drawings from this period are signed and dated by H. D. Stone.

Someone in Windsor—probably Howe and Stone together—developed an early turret lathe. Working at this lathe, a machinist could perform one cutting task after another, simply by shifting a lever that rotated successive tools into position. He could cut the correct thread on a screw, shape the point, cut it off at the proper length, and then begin to thread the next screw without ever having to stop and change the cutting tool or move the workpiece on the machine. It would be just this sort of efficiency that would accelerate production for the Civil War.[17]

Rifling machine made by
Robbins & Lawrence in
Windsor, Vermont, 1863,
collection of American
Precision Museum.
Photo by First Light Studios.

By 1861, the Robbins & Lawrence Company had failed, and the building had passed through several owners. The founders had all gone their separate ways. Lawrence was in Hartford, Connecticut, running the Sharps rifle factory; Nicanor Kendall had retired; and Samuel Robbins had found other interests. Frederick Howe had gone to Providence, where he would spend the war years at Providence Tool Company, and where he would later become president of Brown & Sharpe. Other Robbins & Lawrence alumni were at Colt, Remington, and the Springfield Armory. But Henry Stone had remained in Windsor, raising his children, serving his community, and superintending the peacetime work in the former Robbins & Lawrence factory. In 1861, at the age of 46, he was running the shop.

When the shooting began, the owners were Lamson, Goodnow & Yale. Based in Shelburne Falls, Massachusetts, these manufacturers of scythes and cutlery had developed an interest in machine tools, purchased the armory at a bargain price, and then added sewing machines to their product line.

Ebenezer Lamson, who was responsible for the firm's operations in Windsor, happened also to be a fervent abolitionist. His son, E. E. Lamson, wrote that their home in Shelburne Falls had been "a station on the underground railroad": "Sometimes I would find at our breakfast table a negro whom I had never seen before," he wrote in his memoir. "How or when he arrived or departed, and whither, I never inquired or knew. But I somehow understood that they were on the way to Canada and I hoped they would arrive."[18]

12

Ebenezer G. Lamson,
collection of American
Precision Museum.

In the spring of 1861, there would be no question
about which side Lamson was on. Recognizing the value of
the resources in the former Robbins & Lawrence armory, he
sold off the sewing machine business to Thomas White, and
he set Henry Stone to work restoring and retooling the
machinery for the transition back to gun making. Lamson

13

also traveled to Washington, where he secured a contract for 50,000 rifles. He built a stockade fence around the entire factory complex, and together he and Stone began recruiting a larger work force.[19]

Experienced gun makers, young machinists, and apprentices were recruited not only from the local community, but from machining centers in New Hampshire and Massachusetts—perhaps even farther away, since Stone's network of colleagues extended at least as far as Connecticut and Rhode Island. On September 28, 1861, the *Vermont Journal* reported the upswing in activity at the largest factory in Windsor: "We understand that Lamson, Goodnow & Yale are soon to employ a force of three hundred men in the manufacture of arms, at the Windsor armory, and that as soon as the gas fixtures are put in, the machinery is to run day and night."[20]

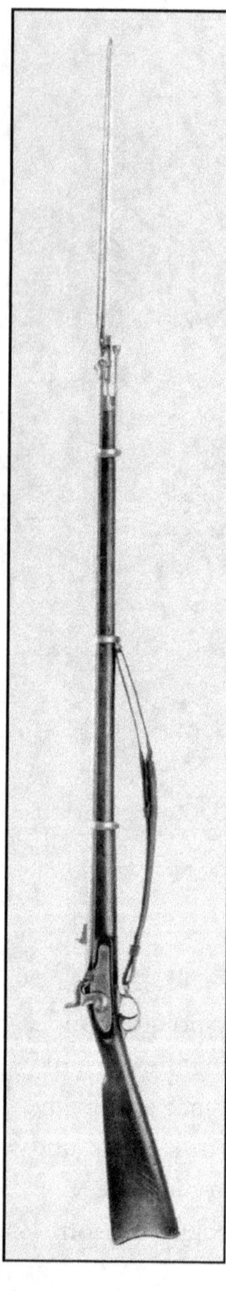

Special Model 1861 rifle-musket, made by Lamson, Goodnow & Yale in Windsor, Vermont. The company produced 50,000 of these weapons.
Photo courtesy of the Shelburne Museum.

The "arms" referred to in the newspaper report were Lamson's contracted 50,000 Special Model 1861 rifle-muskets. A variation of the more common Model 1861 made by the Springfield Armory, the Special Model seems to have been designed at the Colt factory. It resembled the Enfield rifle that had been made in Windsor in the 1850s; and so it would have seemed a familiar and straightforward project

The Windsor armory complex, around 1865.
The tall building with the cupola, at the right rear, now houses
the American Precision Museum.
Photo from a stereograph, courtesy of the University of Vermont.

to Stone and the other Robbins & Lawrence veterans, as they retooled the factory. They had made rifles by the thousands before, and they had made rifles under the pressure of immediate military needs, for the Mexican War and for the Crimean War. If the Union Army would need more than a million rifles, and if the Windsor armory was to run shifts around the clock, why did they produce only 50,000 guns over the course of three years? The company's sales ledgers, analyzed alongside accepted production figures for the major military gun contractors, tell the story.[21]

In August, ten milling machines and one four-spindle machine for drilling out gun barrels went to the Starr Arms Company in Binghamton, New York. Later Starr would order a pistol rifling machine, drill presses, profile milling machines, and screw machines. Starr would make 32,000 Army revolvers between 1863 and 1865.

The Sharps Rifle plant in Hartford also placed orders that August. Sharps ultimately would provide about 20,000 rifles and 80,000 carbines (essentially, a carbine is a short rifle) to the Army and Navy, including 2,000 rifles to outfit the famous Berdan's Sharpshooters.[22]

A young machinist from Massachusetts, William Hale Foster, arrived about this time expecting to work on the government gun contract. In a letter to his wife, who had stayed behind while he looked for lodgings for the family, Foster noted his surprise at what kind of work was actually most needed in Windsor: "I found things different from what I expected in regard to guns. Although the company have taken a contract as reported they will not strike a blow on

Harper's Weekly illustration showing the gun-making operations at Springfield Armory, September 21, 1861, collection of American Precision Museum.

guns for two or three months as it will take that time to get ready. Then they will make only a part of them here. The barrels, bayonets and trimmings are to be made at Northampton, Mass. The locks and stocks will probably be made here. The help that are here now will not have any thing to do on them as they have got all they can do and more to make the machinery for this and other companies."[23]

Foster also noted the long twelve-hour days, the close attention of the supervisor in his department, and the relentless pace of the work: "the man that I work for…is a very good employer but he makes us work every minute of the time. I never worked where every body worked so steady as they do in his room."[24] There was good reason for that

William Hale Foster and his wife, Maria Foster, around 1860.
Photo courtesy of the descendants of William and Maria.

hectic pace. After the Union disaster at Bull Run in July 1861, the government had to acknowledge that the war would not be won quickly, and that the Federal armories would not be able to produce enough arms and ammunition.[25] As the Ordnance Department placed large orders with private gun contractors, many of those contractors were turning to Windsor for the latest in gun-making machinery.

In September, a machine order came in from Remington: milling machines, rifling machines, barrel polishing machines, and more. Remington would produce 40,000 Springfield Model 1861 rifle-muskets, 12,000 "Zouave" rifles, and nearly 30,000 military revolvers. John Walter has calculated that Remington produced 35 percent of Federal handguns.[26] Frederick Howe at the Providence Tool Company also began to place orders in September: machine castings, milling and boring machines, and a complete set of machinery for making wooden gunstocks. Under his leadership, Providence Tool would make 70,000 Model 1861 rifle-muskets.

The growing power of the Federal war machine was reflected in the sights, sounds, and smells of the factory itself: the deep rumble of the great water wheel that powered the overhead line shafts and ran the machinery, or of the coal-fired steam engine that powered the factory when there was too little water in Mill Brook; the closer rumble of the overhead line shafts, and the slapping of the leather belts; the screech of metal cutting metal; the smell of machine oil, gas lamps, tobacco, and sweat. Some of the machines were massive; others had delicate mechanisms; all had heavy cast iron bases to keep them steady and inflexible. Massive castings were produced at the foundry across Main Street, and finished tools were shipped out by rail.

But the atmosphere was not all brawn; the brain was involved as well. The men who designed, built, and operated these machines were the high-tech workers of their day. The designers needed to understand the geometry of a bevel gear, the characteristics of different kinds of steel, how to mill the flutes on a twist drill, and how to create a particular screw thread by controlling the length and speed of the feed mechanism and the angle of the cutting tool. They had to figure out how to design a machine that would be more accurate than its individual parts.

The operator also needed both skill and great care. He had to set up and service his machine. He needed to know how to place a cutting tool just right, and how to keep it sharp, so that the parts produced would all be the same, hour after hour and day after day. William Foster wrote to his wife about the exacting standards at the armory: "They are more particular about their work here than in shops that I have been used to work in. I think that I can do it with a little extra pains."[27]

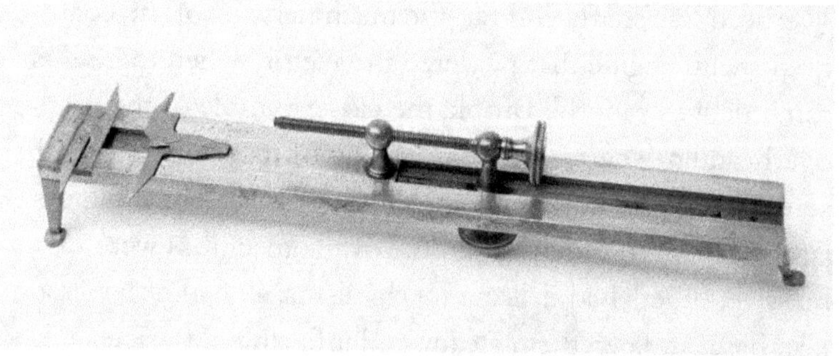

In October 1861, an order came in from Richardson & Overman, a Philadelphia company that would make nearly 18,000 Gallager Carbines. They wanted a variety of machines, including a "letting-in" machine with a 7 ½-foot bed, to be completed in six weeks. The price would be $600, but there would be a bonus of $50 for each week trimmed off the delivery time. In November, Eli Whitney, Jr. began ordering machinery, and the Burnside Rifle Company ordered two milling machines for making a gun designed by General Ambrose E. Burnside.

It was also in November of 1861 that Lamson, Goodnow & Yale began to help transform the Amoskeag Manufacturing Company (AMC) from a textile mill into a gun maker. Established in 1807 in what is now Manchester, New Hampshire, Amoskeag had grown to become one of the largest cotton mills in the country. After the Civil War, it would become perhaps the largest in the world. But in the spring of 1861, when supplies of southern cotton dried up, the company determined to make guns. The AMC "agent" (plant manager), Ezekiel Straw, traveled to Windsor in July and persuaded a former New Hampshire man, Carlos Clark, to leave LG&Y and take charge of the arms operation at Amoskeag.[28] Straw also began planning to purchase machinery and tools from the Windsor firm. Though AMC

Left: Vernier caliper, 1846, unknown maker, collection of American Precision Museum. Photo by First Light Studios.

Capable of reading to thousandths of an inch, the vernier caliper had become a standard tool for machinist in the 1850s.

had a well-equipped machine shop of its own, the rigid standards of a military contract were new to them. The contract with the Ordnance Department specified that the rifles must be "in all respects identical with the standard rifled musket made at the United States Armory at Springfield, Massachusetts and are to interchange with it and each other in all their parts."[29] In the end, Amoskeag arranged to make the same Special Model 1861 rifle that was being made in Windsor, and relied on LG&Y for their gun-making machinery. In addition to machine tools, LG&Y also produced the gauges that would allow constant checking of dimensions, to ensure that all parts would interchange, whether made in Windsor, in Manchester, or at the Colt armory in Hartford.[30] Apparently there was only one model gun, shared among the three armories, and its parts were sent around by "Express" as each factory needed to see them.[31]

Lamson, Goodnow & Yale's first big order from Amoskeag came on November 20, 1861: a profile milling machine; a nut boring machine; a barrel trimming machine; rifling, milling, and screw-making machines. More orders would follow in February and March of 1862. Eventually, the AMC machine shop began making its own machines, using LG&Y patterns and castings. Amoskeag's own records show that they also purchased machinery and measuring tools from Brown & Sharpe and lathes from Putnam Machine. They purchased some gun sights and bayonets from others, as well.[32] But the LG&Y ledger shows us that bayonets purchased by AMC from Bay State Hardware were made on LG&Y machines, and were held together with screws purchased from Lamson, Goodnow & Yale.[33] And so the

22

Revolving tool holder from Lamson, Goodnow turret lathe, made in 1861, collection of American Precision Museum.
Photo by First Light Studios.

Originally, the designers called this a "screw milling machine." During the Civil War, new ironclad warships were topped with powerful gun turrets. Revolving-head lathes soon became known as turret lathes.

Windsor influence came to Amoskeag from several directions. In all, AMC produced 27,000 Special Model rifles in just under two years.[34]

As the dual businesses of making guns and making machinery heated up, Ebenezer Lamson summoned his son, Eastburne, to help out. Eastburne later recalled that, "sometime in the winter of 1861 I, being then a sophomore at Brown University, was informed that the country needed my services, and father my help, in arming our soldiers. Some of my college mates had already left college to join their friends in the army." Eastburne went first to Shelburne Falls and then to Windsor, working as his father's private secretary.

The young man seems to have had a greater interest in rifles than in machine tool sales: "The completion of special tools and fixtures took some months after my arrival. Then followed the real work of gun making and deliveries of rifles, at first 1000 at intervals of two or three weeks, then at shorter intervals—ten days—seven days—until the musket contracts were completed."[35]

January 1862 brought another large request from Richard Lawrence at the Sharps Rifle plant. He wanted a four-spindle drill press, an index milling machine, one or two smooth boring machines, and castings for nine other machines that he would finish in Hartford. The Sharps carbine was in desperately short supply. Since no carbines at all were produced in the Federal armories,[36] all Union carbines had to be produced by private contractors. LG&Y sold equipment not just to Sharps, but to other carbine makers as well: Massachusetts Arms, Burnside, Starr Arms, and Savage.

The year 1862 also brought orders from the Springfield Armory's Major Dyer, who needed forgings, a rifling machine, and a machine for cutting breech pins. Smith & Wesson ordered milling machines, rifling machines, and half a dozen lathes. E. Robinson in New York had a contract for 30,000 Model 1861 rifle-muskets, and he needed milling machines, a drill press, and equipment for making breech pins. Alfred Jenks & Sons, who produced more than 98,000 of the Model 1861 rifle, ordered a profile milling machine. The American Firearms Company of New York placed an order that came to nearly $4,000. Elisha Root at the Colt factory in Hartford ordered machine castings. Other pistol

24

makers also placed orders: J. Stevens & Company in
Chicopee Falls; C. R. Alsop of Middletown, Connecticut; and
the Connecticut Arms Company.

Colt Model 1860 Army Revolver,
collection of American Precision Museum.
Photo by First Light Studios.

According to Merritt Roe Smith, the buildup of gun-
making capacity in the north took about eighteen months:
"By the fall of 1862, most of the Union's needs for arms were
being met by the Springfield Armory and twenty-four private
contractors headed by Colt, Alfred Jenks of Philadelphia, and
the Providence Tool Company of Rhode Island."[37] While the
Lamson, Goodnow & Yale records show Jenks, Colt, and the
Springfield Armory making only a few purchases, the ledgers
demonstrate that most of the other contractors—including
the Providence Tool Company—relied heavily on the
Windsor machine tool firm. Altogether, as many as one-third
of the Model 1861 rifle-muskets were made at factories with a
large number of LG&Y machines, and the vast majority were
made at facilities that had one or more. Add to that, tens of

thousands of carbines, pistols, and bayonets made on LG&Y machines, and the impact of the Windsor firm becomes clear.

The men at Lamson, Goodnow &Yale (and as far as we know the employees were all men) had more on their minds than turning out machine tools and rifles. Henry Stone was also one of the town's selectmen, and so he had responsibility for ensuring that Windsor filled its quota of soldiers. By the summer of 1862, the war was a year old and many Vermonters had already enlisted, answering the first call in 1861. When "Father Abraham" called for 300,000 more in the summer of 1862, Vermont's quota was nearly 5,000 men. Some were to be "nine months men"; others would need to sign up for three years. If the states could not raise enough volunteers, the Federal Militia Act of 1862 would require a draft. Vermont's draft was scheduled to begin in September,[38] but many Vermonters felt that a draft would bring disgrace to the state as well as to the individual town. And so the pressure was on to find volunteers.

At town meeting in Windsor, the selectmen were authorized to borrow "a sum not to exceed $3000 for the purpose of paying one hundred dollars to each member of the uniform militia"[39] —but only to those who volunteered before the need for a draft kicked in. The "war meetings" were held in the town hall. Large crowds gathered; prominent men made patriotic speeches; the town cornet band played. According to the *Vermont Journal,* "the ladies were present in goodly numbers, manifesting the spirit of the mothers of seventy-six, in this critical juncture of our nation."[40]

Unidentified Vermont
soldier, courtesy of the
Library of Congress.

While the guidelines for the draft allowed for some
exemptions, merely working in a war industry job was not
among them. And so the men at the armory were under just
as much pressure to enlist as anyone else. At least three of the
armory's machinists, and possibly more, answered the call
that summer.

William Hale Foster was among the first to come
forward. Twenty-six years old, the father of two little boys, he
had been in Windsor only a year. Early in his stay, he had
commented to Maria that Windsor was "a very patriotic
place,"[41] and he found himself caught up in that patriotism in
August. Charles F. Butman, another machinist, was just

twenty-one and enlisted that same night. Ezra Parker enlisted a month later, and he would become Foster's tent mate in Virginia. Selectman Henry Stone would have been there watching the young men enlist—his neighbors, perhaps some relatives, and men whose work he supervised at the armory. How he felt about sending them off to war, we cannot know. But off they went.

By October, the 12th Regiment had finished its training in Brattleboro and headed for Washington. According to the *Vermont Journal*, the 1,004 men of the 12th were "fully equipped and armed with the Springfield gun."[42] Certainly Foster, Butman, and Parker knew they had had a hand in making those guns.

Foster became ill and was discharged that winter. Butman and Parker survived the war without injury, as their unit saw very little action. As the months and years wore on, other Windsor men were not so fortunate. Samuel Fitch was wounded at the Wilderness; Joseph Bickford at Cold Harbor. Thomas Little, an African American from West Windsor, served with the 54th Massachusetts and survived the disastrous assault on Fort Wagner, but was discharged with some sort of disability right at the end of the war.[43]

Other Windsor men did not make it through. Horace Houghton was wounded at Lee's Mill in April 1862, survived his wounds, then died of disease six months later. Thomas Ensworth was wounded at the Wilderness and died after two days of suffering. William Carter Tracy was killed in action in Virginia in 1864. As Henry Stone and the workmen at LG&Y were shipping out crates of machine tools and boxes of rifles, these local boys were coming home in wooden boxes. Other soldiers never made it home at all. Charles Gleason, James

Left, "Battle of Chancellorsville, Sunday May 3, 1863," from *Frank Leslie's Illustrated History of the Civil War,* 1895.
On May 5, as the Union army retreated, Vermont troops protected the rear. Total casualties, North and South, were nearly 30,000 during the Chancellorsville Campaign.

Stone, and Silas Worthing died at Andersonville Prison. Joseph A. Smith, killed at Petersburg, was buried at Flower's farm. Richard Rich died at Cedar Creek and was buried in Winchester. Henry Marsh was buried in North Carolina.[44]

As the lists of dead and wounded arrived and as the newspaper reported victories and defeats on the battlefield, the work of the factory went on. September 1863 brought orders from Smith & Wesson, Remington, Providence Tool, Sharps Rifle, and many others. Original shop drawings at the American Precision Museum, dated 1864, show new fixtures that were being designed for the profile milling machine—to shape triggers, hammers, and lock plates.[45]

In January 1863, in the midst of this frantic production of guns and gun-making machinery, Henry Stone's six-year-old son died of croup. One year later, his wife, Julia, died of pneumonia.[46] She left him with three children—a fourteen-year-old boy from his first marriage, and two little ones under the age of four.

Through much of 1864, the work remained relentless. There were now some 400 men on hand, running machinery around the clock.[47] Even before the original contract for 50,000 rifles was complete, Ebenezer Lamson had turned his sights on newer, more modern guns. The next big advances in military small arms would be breech-loading and repeating weapons. Loading the gun at the breech, rather than ramming the bullet down the far end of the muzzle, allowed soldiers to reload while lying on the ground, or crouching behind a breastwork, or mounted on a horse. Midway through the war, Lamson brought in William Palmer and Colonel Hiram

Berdan to work on new designs for breech-loading carbines.
Lamson had also purchased Albert Ball's patent for a
repeating gun magazine and brought Ball to Windsor to
design a repeating carbine for use by the cavalry. In February
1864, a representative from the factory went to Washington
with a sample of a repeating rifle that could fire ten charges in
rapid succession.[48] As a result of these efforts, Lamson
received government orders for 1,000 Ball carbines and 1,000
Palmer carbines.[49] Ball took charge of manufacturing guns,[50]
while Henry Stone remained busy with the machines that
made gun parts.

The autumn of 1864 brought the war even closer to
home and increased the level of stress at the armory. On
October 19, a small group of Confederate soldiers—who had
crossed into Vermont from Canada a few days earlier—
staged a raid on St. Albans, robbing three banks, killing one
civilian, wounding several others, and attempting—but
failing—to burn down the town. The citizens of Vermont

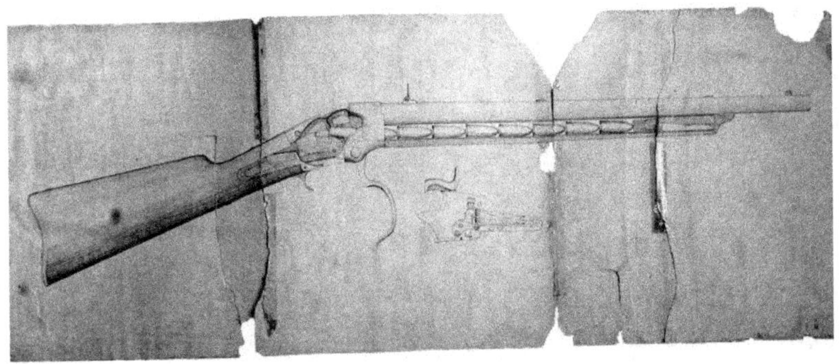

Drawing of the Ball Repeating Carbine,
collection of American Precision Museum.

were instructed to organize militias for the defense of their towns and to watch out for vagrants.[51] A small band of raiders could never carry off Windsor's cast iron and steel machine tools, but the factory itself might have been seen as a target. Earlier that year, one of the main buildings at the Colt armory in Hartford had burned down, destroying a thousand lathes and milling machines and throwing 900 men out of work[52] Though no one seriously suspected sabotage, it was mentioned as a possibility. And then there were the LG&Y guns that might be stolen, Special Model rifles as well as the two new carbines. Guards around the armory were increased, and they patrolled day and night.[53] The extra precautions, however, proved unnecessary. No more Confederate raids followed the one in St. Albans.

During the winter of 1864-65, work at the armory began to slow. It was around that time that Lamson bought out his partners, Goodnow and Yale, and reorganized as E. G. Lamson & Company. Under that name, the last few Special Model rifles were completed, along with the Ball and Palmer contracts. Because most of the other arms makers were now fully equipped, machine sales were light. Some spare rifle parts went to the arsenal in Washington: barrels, gunstocks, lock plates, hammers, screws, springs, bridles, and butt plates. The Rollin White Arms Company bought a pistol rifling machine. Thomas White ordered some more sewing machine parts. In March, samples of the Ball and Palmer guns were shipped to an Ordnance Department inspector in New York for final approval. In April, Union troops occupied Richmond, and Lee surrendered at Appomattox. By the end of May, the war was over. There would be no more gun contracts from the government, and the market for gun-making machinery evaporated.

Ebenezer Lamson, now fifty-one years old, was not a man to give up or to retire early. By January 1866, he was sending samples of saw mill equipment to companies in Kentucky, Georgia, and Texas. His nephew, Ralph H. Lamson, who had served as an officer in the Navy and had great success capturing blockade runners, took on the task of trying to persuade governments on the other side of the Atlantic—the English, the French, the Prussians, the Danes—to order Palmer and Ball rifles. Colt's Patent Firearms ordered 2,000 gunstocks and assorted breech screws and springs, perhaps for use on the guns they were making for the Russian government. Although Colt had sales in Russia, and Remington was selling excess carbines to France, young Ralph Lamson had little success interesting anyone in the Ball and Palmer guns.

Typically, E. G. Lamson had many other projects to take his mind off the disappointing gun sales. He was busy building up an inventory of peacetime products: forging machinery, saw mills, hand tools, general purpose machine tools, and another sewing machine. He also had Albert Ball working on a stone-channeling machine for quarry work. Unfortunately, that project led to a long, expensive, and painful patent dispute. When it became clear that Lamson would lose the lawsuit, Ball moved across the river to New Hampshire and helped found Sullivan Machine. In 1869, Lamson formed a partnership with Russell Jones, a textile manufacturer from Massachusetts, who turned the original 1846 armory building into a cotton mill. Eventually, Lamson's health was crippled and his fortune diminished by the business struggles of the 1870s and '80s. He moved to Boston and then to Martha's Vineyard, where would die in 1891.

As others drifted away, Henry David Stone remained, ever faithful to Windsor and to the old Robbins & Lawrence armory. Five months after the war ended, he married again. Laura Emmons Sylvester was a thirty-one-year-old widow when they married, and she helped raise Henry's children. She was active in church and charity work, and she was known in town as "the central figure of a bright and happy home."[54] Henry worked on more sewing machine designs as well as machine tool improvements. During the cotton mill period, he continued to supervise the Jones, Lamson & Company machine division in the shops on the other side of Mill Brook. In 1874, Stone received a patent for an improved power feed mechanism for the slide on turret lathes.[55]

By 1888, the company had been weakened by the failure of the cotton mill and by the stone-channeler lawsuit, and it needed an infusion of cash. Investors from Springfield, Vermont, came forward, purchased the company, and moved most of its assets, by oxcart, twenty miles to the south.[56] When James Hartness arrived at Jones & Lamson, in 1889, the Howe/Stone turret lathe was still in use. Building upon that machine, Hartness soon developed a much improved, flat turret lathe that became the basis for the growth of Jones & Lamson into one of the machine tool powerhouses of the twentieth century.[57] Most certainly, the achievements of what came to be called "Precision Valley" were based upon the pioneering work of the men at the old Robbins & Lawrence armory, both before and during the Civil War.

Stone did not go along to Springfield. He was seventy-three years old and, again, he had an ill wife. Laura died in August 1889. Henry would live another eleven years. His long life had seen a good deal of sorrow: He had been widowed three times, had buried three of his five children, and had helped send dozens of his townsmen off to war. More than twenty of them did not return. A Lincoln Republican and a patriot, working for an abolitionist employer, he probably had no regrets about his role in arming the Federal troops. It is one of the eternal ironies of war that

Henry David Stone, collection of American Precision Museum.

good people, doing what they perceive to be their duty, can help create such pain and tragedy. At the end of Henry Stone's life, he was remembered as a leader in his community—a stabilizing force at the town's largest factory, a selectman, a member of the school board, a director on the board of the local bank, a prominent member of the Masonic Lodge, and always an advocate for technological progress. In 1881, he had been one of the first people in town to put a street lamp in front of his home on Main Street.[58]

There had been many other inventive minds at the armory during the war, in addition to Stone, Ball, and Palmer. One D.M. Moore had developed a ratchet wrench that saw its first use in Windsor. He patented it in 1864 and then moved on to other towns and other inventions.[59] Quimby Backus invented a bench vise, a bit brace, and an adjustable wrench. Later in life, he would develop a steam radiator and gas logs. William Henry Barber was also working at the armory in Windsor when he patented his bit brace with spring-loaded, adjustable jaws. George Henry Coates had entered the armory as a fourteen-year-old apprentice in 1863. A local boy, he stayed on a few years after the war, until he became a journeyman machinist in 1869. Later, at Ethan Allen Firearms, he would develop a self-cocking gun. By the end of his career, Coates held forty patents and owned a large company that made a variety of tools.

Such was the talent pool in Windsor during the war. In other shops, linked to Windsor through training, business, friendship, and competition, machinists were doing similar work: at Colt, Providence Tool Company, Ames Manufacturing, the Springfield Armory, and other tool- and gun-making centers, machines were built and improved as part of the process of making guns to arm the Union troops.

As Allen Yale has pointed out, Henry Stone and his earlier colleagues at Robbins & Lawrence had also—inadvertently—helped arm the Confederacy. Not only were many northern weapons captured on the battlefield by Confederate soldiers, who then put them to deadly use; but also the Confederate government managed to purchase guns from England—made on machinery patterned after the Robbins & Lawrence machine tools sold to the Enfield Armory back in the mid-1850s. Finally, the Confederate States imported gun-making machinery from England—again patterned after those Robbins & Lawrence machines at the Enfield Armory.[60]

Of course the war was neither won nor lost by the producers of guns or gun-making tools. Life and warfare are far too complicated for that. But the size of the armies, the course of the war, and the sheer magnitude of the carnage on the battlefield depended upon the ability of a president, an army, a nation, to put the latest weapons into the hands of more than two million soldiers. And the ability to make weapons by the millions depended upon the quantity production of machine-made interchangeable parts. The Lamson, Goodnow & Yale Company may have produced only 50,000 rifles, but they provided the machinery—precise, reliable, state-of-the-art machinery—that made it possible for other contractors to produce well over a million weapons, made to exacting military specifications.

The machine technology created for warfare in the nineteenth century—like much military technology in the twentieth century—would later be used to deliver a profusion of consumer goods, including ready-to-wear clothing, factory-canned foods, bicycles, home appliances, and automobiles. The Civil War itself brought profound changes to American politics, government, and society. It is often said that the war shaped a new nation, created a new concept of America. The men at the armory in Windsor, led by Henry Stone and Ebenezer Lamson, helped shape the war itself.

Lamson Iron Planer, 1864, collection of American Precision Museum. Photo by First Light Studios

END NOTES

[1] Drew Gilpin Faust, *This Republic of Suffering: Death and the American Civil War* (New York: Alfred A. Knopf, 2008), 66.

[2] Ibid., xi, 188.

[3] James M. McPherson, *Battle Cry of Freedom: The Civil War Era* (New York: Oxford University Press, 1988), 485, 487.

[4] See, for example, Faust, *This Republic of Suffering*, 4, 41; McPherson, *Battle Cry of Freedom*, 475.

[5] Major Richard D. Moorehead, "Technology and the American Civil War," *Military Review* (June 2004): 61.

[6] See, for example, Earl J. Hess, *The Rifle Musket in Civil War Combat: Reality and Myth* (Lawrence: University Press of Kansas, 2008); Paddy Griffith, *Battle Tactics of the Civil War* (New Haven: Yale University Press, 2001).

[7] Richard A. Gabriel and Karen S. Metz, "The Dawn of Modern War," accessed December 9, 2009, http://www.au.af.mil/au/awc/awcgate/gabrmetz/gabr001b.htm; Moorehead, "Technology and the American Civil War."

[8] Faust, *This Republic of Suffering*, 3. Estimates vary, but Faust uses the figures 2.1 million northerners and 880,000 southerners. By contrast, she notes that "During the American Revolution the army never numbered more than 30,000 men."

[9] Carl L. Davis, *Arming the Union: Small Arms in the Civil War* (Port Washington, N.Y.: National University Publications, Kennikat Press, 1973), vii; McPherson, *Battle Cry of Freedom*, 475.

[10] Norm Flayderman, *Flayderman's Guide to Antique American Firearms...and their values*, 8th ed. (Iola, Wisc.: Gun Digest Books, 2001), 465.

[11] Richard Colton, "Arms of the Confederacy," Springfield Armory National Historic Site, accessed September 22, 2010, http://www.nps.gov/spar, p. 2.

[12] For examples of previous scholarly commentary on "levels of weapons production never before imagined" see Gabriel and Metz, "The Dawn of Modern War"; Pauline Maier, Merritt Roe Smith, and Alexander Keyssar, *Inventing America*, 2nd ed., vol. 1 (New York: W. W. Norton, 2005): 504.

[13] There is much strong scholarship on the topic of the early spread of machining practice. See, for example, Felicia Johnson Deyrup, *Arms Makers of the Connecticut Valley: A Regional Study of the Economic Development of the Small Arms Industry, 1798-1870*, vol. 33, Smith College Studies in History (Northampton, Ma., 1948); David R. Meyer, *Networked Machinists: High-Technology Industries in Antebellum America* (Baltimore: Johns Hopkins University Press, 2006); Merritt Roe Smith, *Harpers*

Ferry Armory and New Technology: The Challenge of Change (Ithaca, N.Y.: Cornell University Press, 1977).

[14] "Records of Sharps Rifle Company, 1852-1898," various letters, 1855, Connecticut Historical Society.

[15] This design is credited to Stone in U. S. Department of Interior, *Fire-Arms Manufacture 1880*, rpt. 1992 (U.S. Government Printing Office, 1883), 29. The reference to "the English gun" comes from a shop drawing for a lock plate stud milling machine, signed by Stone, dated July 1855, in the collection of the American Precision Museum.

[16] U. S. Department of Interior, *Fire-Arms Manufacture 1880*, 66.

[17] The idea of the turret lathe may have originated in England, and Frederick Howe had probably seen such a machine at the Silver & Gay company in Massachusetts, before he moved to Windsor. Howe and Stone actually got a turret machine working sometime around 1850 and began to sell it to other gun makers. Deyrup, *Arms Makers of the Connecticut Valley*, 158; Guy Hubbard, *Windsor Industrial History* (Windsor, Vt.: The Town School District, 1922), 100-101; U. S. Department of Interior, *Fire-Arms Manufacture 1880*, 68.

[18] Eastsburne E. Lamson, "Ebenezer Goodnow Lamson," memoir written in Salt Lake City, Utah, August 1912, copy in the library of the Vermont Historical Society, 7.

[19] Hubbard, *Windsor Industrial History*, 129.

[20] *Vermont Journal*, 28 September 1861, 8.

[21] Numbers of weapons produced by the various companies listed below come from Flayderman, *Flayderman's Guide*.

[22] Flayderman, *Flayderman's Guide*, 170; see also "The Sharps," accessed March 1, 2011, http://www.civilwarhome.com/sharps.htm; "CIVIL WAR SMALL-ARMS," accessed March 11, 2011, http://www.nps.gov/archive/gett/soldierlife/webguns.htm.

[23] Letters of William Hale Foster and Maria Foster, 9 August 1861, private collection.

[24] William Hale Foster to Maria Foster, 21 August 1861.

[25] Davis, *Arming the Union*, iv, vi.

[26] John Walter, *The Guns that Won the West: Firearms on the American Frontier, 1848-1898* (London: Greenhill Books, 1999), 95.

[27] William Hale Foster to Maria Foster, 9 August 1861.

[28] "Carlos D. Clark, Inventor," *Manchester Mirror*, 19 October 1894, clipping in the collection of the Manchester Historic Association.

[29] Warren H. Hay, "U.S. Amoskeag," *The Gun Report*, 14 (June 1968): 11-12.

[30] Ibid., 12.

40

31 "Amoskeag Machine Company Letter Book," vol. 15: 469, Manchester Historic Association Research Center. The gauges that were being shuttled around are mentioned in vol. 16: 6, in a letter dated 18 June 1862.

32 Ibid., 5: 87, 79, 95.

33 Amoskeag purchase of bayonets appears in "AMC Machine Shop Cash Book 1861-68," vol. 5, March 1863, 79, Manchester Historic Association Research Center. LG&Y sale of bayonets and bayonet clasp screws to Bay State Hardware appears in the LG&Y order book at American Precision Museum, entries for April 1862 and January 1863.

34 Flayderman, *Flayderman's Guide*, 468; Hay, "U.S. Amoskeag," 13.

35 Lamson, "Ebenezer Goodnow Lamson," 13.

36 Davis, *Arming the Union*, vi-vii.

37 Maier, Smith, and Keyssar, *Inventing America*, 1: 504.

38 *Vermont Journal*, 16 August 1862, 5 and 8; Douglas Harper, "The Northern Draft of 1862," accessed September 23, 2010, http://www.etymonline.com/cw/draft.htm.

39 *Vermont Journal*, 6 September 1862, 8.

40 Ibid., 13 September 1862, 8.

41 William Hale Foster to Maria Foster, 18 August 1861.

42 *Vermont Journal*, 11 October 1862, 8.

43 Service records for men credited to Vermont are available at http://vermontcivilwar.org.

44 Information on which Windsor soldiers are buried in Windsor and which are buried in the south comes from "Vermont in the Civil War," http://vermontcivilwar.org/index/index.php.

45 Drawings of these fixtures, dated May 1864, in the flat files at American Precision Museum.

46 *Vermont Journal*, 30 January 1864, 8; Town of Windsor Vital Records, Book 4, 41.

47 Leander Bishop, *A History of American Manufactures from 1608 to 1860* (Philadelphia: Sampson, Low, Son & Co., 1864), 691, accessed via http://books.google.com/books.

48 *Vermont Journal*, 27 February 1864, 8.

49 Hubbard, *Windsor Industrial History*, 129-30; Lamson, "Ebenezer Goodnow Lamson," 13; Bishop, *History of American Manufactures*, 690-91; Walter, *Guns that Won the West*, 89-90; Flayderman, *Flayderman's Guide*, 506, 517.

50 Walter, *Guns that Won the West*, 89; Hubbard, *Windsor Industrial History*, 129.

51 *Vermont Journal*, 12 November 1864.

52 "The Fire at Colt's Armory," *New York Times*, 7 February 1864.

[53] *Vermont Journal,* 29 October 1864, 8; Hubbard, *Windsor Industrial History,* 127.

[54] *Vermont Journal,* 10 August 1889, obituary for Laura Stone.

[55] Hubbard, *Windsor Industrial History,* 137.

[56] "Hartness House--History, Observatory and Museum--Springfield Vermont Historical Landmark," accessed December 7, 2010, http://www.hartnesshouse.com/hartness-history.shtml.

[57] Joseph W. Roe, *English and American Tool Builders,* rpt.1987 (New Haven: Yale University Press, 1916), 197-99; "The Hartness Mansion," http://www.hartnesshouse.com/hartness-history.shtml.

[58] *The Valley Farmer,* 17 December 1881, 7.

[59] Randy Roeder, "Millers Falls Bit Braces: Barber, Amidon, Parsons, etc.," accessed September 23, 2010, http://oldtoolheaven.com/brace/FeaturedBraces.htm.

[60] Allen Yale, "Vermonters Who Helped Arm the Confederacy: A Case of Unintended Consequences" (paper presented to the Civil War Roundtable, Newport, Vermont, March 2009, copy courtesy of the author); Roe, *English and American Tool Builders,* 140; Colton, *Arms of the Confederacy.* For more on sources of Confederate gun-making equipment, see Smith, *Harpers Ferry Armory and New Technology,* 320-22. For documentation of the number of tools that went from Robbins & Lawrence to Enfield, see Nathan Rosenberg, ed., *The American System of Manufactures: The Report of the Committee on the Machinery of the United States 1855 and the Special Reports of George Wallis and Joseph Whitworth 1854* (Edinburgh: Edinburgh University Press, 1969), 182-85.

Front cover: Battle of Franklin, Tennessee, November 30, 1864.
Kurz & Allison Chromolithograph, 1891, courtesy of the Library of Congress.

Turret Lathe, collection of American Precision Museum.
Photo by First Light Studios.

A Note from the Museum

Carrie Brown's essay *Arming the Union* grew out of her research for the museum's new interpretive plan. With partial funding from the National Endowment for the Humanities, APM is developing a new 4,000- square foot exhibition exploring the history of precision manufacturing in America—the machines, the innovators, and the workers who have helped shape the world we live in today. The section of that exhibition that covers the Civil War era opened ahead of the rest of the project, in May 2012, as part of our commemoration of the 150th anniversary of the Civil War. Both *Arming the Union* and the larger project, *Shaping America*, reveal a remarkable story that demonstrates the enormous impact of a small factory in Vermont.

Carrie Brown has been affiliated with APM off and on since 1994, serving as consulting curator for eight exhibitions. She holds a Ph.D. from the University of Virginia and is the author of books and articles on many topics, including *Rosie's Mom: Forgotten Women Workers of the First World War*. Her work focuses on finding the human story behind historic events and on exploring the interplay between technology and culture.

The museum is pleased to present *Arming the Union*—both the book and the exhibition—as part of the Civil War Sesquicentennial and as a preview of our upcoming re-interpretation of the site, *Shaping America.*

American Precision Museum
May 2012

www.ingramcontent.com/pod-product-compliance
Lightning Source LLC
Chambersburg PA
CBHW072129150726
47999CB00005B/2213